INTRODUCTION

The poetry in this second volume of *Love Me When I'm Most Unlovable* represents not only my own feelings but those of thousands of teenagers throughout the nation. Thanks to the NASSP *NewsLeader* and *Read* magazine, young people in middle schools and junior high schools submitted more than 5,000 poems to be reviewed for this publication.

In order to allow them to be as open and honest with their feelings, we had promised anonymity. Be assured, however, the sentiments expressed in this book are truly representative of the young people who attend America's middle schools.

All poems were screened by the students of the Mineola Middle School under the direction of their teacher, Ilene Czerniewicz. Their time and dedication are appreciated since thousands of submissions were reduced to fewer than 100 recommendations.

The students of two other schools were also helpful, and we would like to personally acknowledge the contributions of George H. Gilson Jr. High School, Valdez, Alaska and Sul Ross

Middle School, San Antonio, Texas. Their teachers, Larry Garrison and Delia Garza, were able to create the trusting kind of environment that allowed their students to express their deepest feelings honestly.

Kahlil Gibran once said that, "work is love made visible." The children and teachers join me in presenting our love to you.

ON FEELINGS OF JOY AND INSECURITY

My locker has
   dirty gym socks

last week's assignments
   crumpled papers

broken pencils
   dirty kleenex

saxophone reeds
   apple cores

rotten banana peels
   overdue library books

and a lock that will not open

Adult? I ask
Is that what I am?
When I do something good
my parents answer yes.
When I do something bad
my parents answer no.
What am I?
An adult or child?
I am trusted
to watch the house for a day.
But never
a week or weekend.
Am I an adult,
or am I a child?
At the movies
I pay adult admission.
But for rated R films,
I am not admitted.
I ask again,
Is a teenager an adult or child?

There's a time for us in life
that no one understands.
We grow and change in
many ways and later find
out why.

We face new problems
every day and sometimes
it's just so unbearable
We have to break down
and cry.
During these times there
are good and bad
And we hope our parents
will just understand,
For what is happening to us
cannot be controlled,
No matter what we are told.
So bear with us, grow
with us, and learn to
love us through it.

Can they hear what we can hear?
Can they see what we can see?
Can they feel what we can feel?
Pain, sorrow, happiness, joy,
These make up our life
You ask, why don't we give it up?
'Cause there's nothing quite like,
those teenage years

Thirteen ...
What an age!
Christmas just around the corner
Too old for dolls
Too young for high heels
Too old for a fancy red tricycle
Too young for dazzling diamonds
What shall I do?
WISH FOR A CREDIT CARD!

Something must be
wrong with me
In elementary school
I loved when my Mom came
on field trips

And was a big-deal PTA Lady
Now that I'm in Junior High
I get embarrassed
If she comes
near the place.

I wanted to get into an honor class;
My parents warned me my grades would fall,
My classroom teacher told me

she wasn't sure I could take
the competition,
My counselor said the class
was too crowded,
You somehow got them to
open the door.

Should I live with him or her?
I love Mom,
I love Dad.
Why do they have to
get a divorce?
I love Mom,
I love Dad.
Then it must be me!
I'll go away—
I won't hide—
I won't run away—
I won't even stay at a
friend's house—
I'll die. That's it. I'll die!
Hopefully, they'll stay together.
Bye Mom.
Bye Dad.
I love you!

I tried out for chorus
And made it
Now here I am singing
With a hundred other kids
And worrying that everyone
in the audience is only
looking at me.

I prayed to make the
basketball team.
Today's our first game and
I'm sitting on the bench
looking at the crowd.
And praying the coach doesn't
put me in.

Our school taught me
a lot of subjects
But the thing I'll
remember most is
when we
raised the money to help pay
for that kid's plastic surgery.
When we saw him after the operation
it was the greatest feeling in the world
when we cried together.

Everyone is always talking
about sex.
The kids keep passing
around pictures of naked
girls.
I must be crazy
'Cause I go bananas
when she just says hello.

———————

They keep telling us to be mature
If I was mature
I wouldn't be worried about
everything under the sun.
After studying about cancer in Health
I even worry about the sun!

———————

They teach me about drugs,
alcohol, AIDS, and sex,
I wish they'd help me to
get up the nerve to ask Mary
if I could walk her home!

———————

I forgot my French homework
I left my sneakers on the bus
My lunch is in the refrigerator at home
I remembered my speech for English
But when I got up in
front of the class to give it
My teacher told me my
fly was open.

Why do they call art
    a minor subject

When it's the major love of
    my life

It's on my desk but
I live with Mom this week
and left it at Dad's house

In elementary school
I was such a big wheel
In charge of the safety squad
All the little kids looked up to me

I knew everyone in my school
Now I graduated—going to The Middle School
I'm worried
I don't know the kids from the other schools
It's such a big building
I'm nobody again
I don't know if I should wish for the summer
 to end
Or pray for it to go on forever

They tease me when I get
good grades
They tease me because I come to
class prepared
They tease me when I answer
questions in class
They tease me because I carry
pens, notebooks, and texts
Would they respect me if I
carried a knife?

I wish playing the violin
 was cool

I wish getting As
 was cool

I wish being neat
    was cool

It seems you gotta be bad
    to be cool in this school

When I'm on the ballfield
I hope the whole world is
watching.
When I have to make a
speech I wish I could crawl
into a hole.
I seem to be good in things
that people don't think are
important.

If I do my homework
    I'm a nerd

If I get along with teachers
    I'm a nerd

If I play with younger kids
    I'm a nerd

If I don't drink or do drugs
    I'm a nerd

If I don't wear jeans
    I'm a nerd

Maybe being called a nerd is
    sometimes a compliment

I go to the girl's room when
    I come to school
    I put on make up
    Roll up my skirt at the waist
    and even put on some of
    my friend's sexy clothes

If my Mom made a surprise
visit I'd be grounded for
life.

You say I'd like
    symphonies

If I listened to them
    more often

I say you'd like
    rock

If you listened to it
    more often

We're singing in the halls,
Hanging out at the malls,
Even at home
I feel all alone
I don't know what it is
I have to be with kids

My name was called
    on the school's loudspeaker
Everyone stared at me . . .
They thought I played hookey,
    cut a class,
      got into trouble
I acted tough until I got out of
    the room

Then laughed all the way down
    to the office because I
    knew it was just Mom
    bringing me my lunch!

I'm always afraid
They're gonna put me
down because of my hair,
skin, size, or what I'm wearing
When I walk down the hall
I think someone's going to jump
out of a locker and tease me!

I'm too young to go to the
    movies by myself

I'm too young to hang out at
    the Mall

I'm too young to buy my own
    clothes

I mature quite suddenly when I
    have to babysit for my
    darn kid brother

In elementary school I
got all As because I was
neat, did extra reports and
behaved in class.
In the middle school
neatness doesn't count,
projects don't replace test scores,
and behavior doesn't influence grades.
I'm in big trouble!

The things you think of
When you're young
Seem so important
Second to none

The clothes you wear
The lines you speak
The kids you're seen with
Walking down the street

You're classified
In many types
A biker, a nerd
A kicker, a turd

The friends you thought
Were friends in the past,
Are going much further
They're growing so fast

The pressure is high
From those on drugs
You want to say no
To those addicted thugs

This frustrating world
Can make you cry
When those who can succeed
Refuse to try

The poor kids are stoned
The rich kids are high
If I were a bird
I'd fly, fly, fly

To a faraway place
Where trees can be trees
And best of all
I can be me

How many times they give me that eye,
All of a sudden I just want to cry

I want to stand up, I want to speak aloud
I want to do something to make me feel proud

I want to be funny, I want to be smart
I want to be noticed deep down in my heart

How I want to be that girl over there
Everyone likes her, she's never given a stare

She seems so perfect, she does everything right,
Whenever I try, I feel an awful fright!

She can talk to the guys, she can even make jokes
When I try to *talk*, it gets stuck in my throat

My parents both tell me "Just be yourself"
Whenever I do I feel like an elf

One day I'll stand "up"
One day I'll be "proud"
One day I'll feel like I'm part
Of the "crowd"

Teenagers are more
    honest than grownups

Adults say they like the
    stories in the girlie
    magazines

We admit we love the
    pictures

ON PARENTS

Billy has both parents
John's parents are divorced
Mel lives with each parent
　　every other week
Tom lives with his Mom
Sean lives with his Dad
Craig lives with his grandparents
Rich lives with his stepfather
Somebody better re-define family

I bring home my test
proud of my B
"You could do better"
is what they say to me
I jump and run
let out a screech
They say "act your age"
along with a speech
After my game
I sit down and rest
All they could say was
"you didn't try your best"

They expect of me
what I cannot give
and are constantly telling me
How to live
I'm only thirteen
I'm supposed to act wild
But dad says
"*he* wasn't when *he* was a child"

Now living with them
is kind of tough
Especially when nothing
is ever good enough!

———————

If you want to
    scare your parents
    or get them uptight

Talk about
    drugs
    gays
    teenage suicide
    sex
    abortion

If you want to have a
conversation talk about
>   history
>   politics
>   old times
>   sports
>   teachers and
>   school

Mom lives on tranquilizers
Dad smokes like a chimney
Grandma pops valium
>   and they all tell me
>   not to take drugs

Every time I talk to my
friends I say the right thing.

Every time I talk to my
teacher I feel I could have
said it better.

Every time I talk to my
parents I wish I would have
kept my mouth closed.

My parents can't believe
that boys and girls take
gym, home economics, industrial
art and health together.
They must have gone to school
a million years ago.

I have my own room
    computer
    dirt bike
    stereo
    skis
    and VCR
I don't see why they think
it's a good idea for me to
get a paper route.

My parents always
    argue
    smoke
    drink
    and curse
But ask me to be mature

ON TEACHERS

A bad accountant costs
    you some money

A bad lawyer fouls
    up some cases

A bad doctor
    can hurt some patients

A bad teacher
    messes up 125 kids a year

I wish "no pass no play" would go away
    but it's a law that's here to stay.

It's a law that keeps the kids away
    from playing the sports they like to play.

They say for sports we need a C
    but we can pass in class with a D.

What about kids who don't participate?
    Nothing happens to them if their grades
    aren't so great.

What ever happened to the American way?
    I always thought freedom was here to stay.

I never thought people could be so cruel
    as to kick us out of sports in our school.

I'm up at the board
    all ready to go
I'll prove to you all
    just how much I know!

Seven times four
    that's twenty-eight
See, you guys
    I'm doing great!

Now seven times six
    is that twenty-one?
No, it's forty-two
    gosh, I'm dumb!

I'm almost finished
    just one last sum
What! It's wrong!
    Gee how come?

Don't get nervous
    don't start to blush
I've started to shake
    I'm feeling flush!

Oh, how I hate math
    for this reason you see
Sometimes when I'm up here
    they all laugh at me.

I came to you with a problem
    You listened
    You agreed I was right
You told me not to fight the system
    And I began my search
    For a new hero

Why call on me when
I don't know the answer?
I hope it's not for spite.
Don't you know I don't know the answer?
Can't you call on me when I do?

Kids were running in the halls
Teachers were screaming at their classes
The principal was paging the custodian
But your class was great
    like another time zone
    another world.

When a school is a zoo
    the kids act like animals

If the teachers are not in charge
    the kids are wild

It doesn't take a genius to know
    who darn well better run the show

He never cracked a joke

He never allowed us to have
a party before a holiday

He graded every bit of homework

He made us work harder
than any other teacher

I was never so confident
taking a final examination

A great teacher is not always
lovable

Everyone goes crazy in his class
The kids say it's fun
I hate it!
I'm ashamed for him
I can't respect him
I wonder
if he respects himself?

I love when a teacher
praises me,
I can accept when a teacher
is angry,
I hate it when a teacher puts
me down in front
of the class.

It's tough having a
team of teachers.

They talk about me,
They know my good points
and weaknesses,
They know if I'm goofing off.
Even though they try to help me,
I'm not sure I like having
four more parents.

———————

Will you teach me how to sail,
through space upon a comet's tail?
Will you teach me how to fly,
to sail the skies on wings untried?
Will you teach me how to soar,
to see things never seen before?
But most importantly of all,
Will you teach me how to fall?
Will you teach me how to cry,
to release feelings deep inside?
Will you teach me how to laugh,
and travel off the beaten path?
Will you teach me how to dream,
to face the future sight-unseen?
Will you teach me how to be,
the only thing I can be,
me.

———————